Into a Thousand Mouths

Into a Thousand Mouths

Janice Whittington

Texas Tech University Press

The Walt McDonald First-Book Poetry Series

This book was set in Galliard. The paper used in this book meets the minimum requirements of ANSI/NISO Z39.48-1992 (R1997).♾

Design by Melissa Bartz

Printed in the United States of America

Library of Congress Cataloging-in-Publication Data
Whittington, Janice.
    Into a thousand mouths / Janice Whittington.
        p.   cm.
    ISBN 0-89672-413-1 (alk. paper)
    I. Title.
    PS3573.H568I58   1999
    811'.54—dc 21   98-42757
                                              CIP

99 00 01 02 03 04 05 06 07 / 9 8 7 6 5 4 3 2 1

Texas Tech University Press
Box 41037
Lubbock, Texas 79409-1037 USA

800-832-4042

ttup@ttu.edu

Http://www.ttup.ttu.edu

Acknowledgments

I am grateful to the editors of the following publications, in which a number of my poems first appeared:

The Beloit Poetry Journal: "Bloodlines"
Concho River Review: "Highway 36"
Creeping Bent: "The Music of Bones"
Kansas Quarterly: "Expensive Harvest"
Mid-American Review: "Mesquites in February"
Mississippi Valley Review: "Dust and Snow," "Late
    Frost"
The Panhandler: "The Arrowhead"
Southern Poetry Review: "Hailstorm," "What Percent
    Water"
Touchstone: "Storm Watch," "Salt Licks," "Coyote
    Spring," "What It Takes," "Canada Geese in
    Texas," "Storms in Summer"
Writers' Forum: "Winter in a West Texas Town"

"All the Watchers Are Women" first appeared in the
    anthology *Influenced by Light,* and "Does My
    Father Dream of Sons?" was the title poem of my
    chapbook, published by The University of West
    Florida 1990.

I would like to thank Judith Keeling, Melissa Bartz, and others at Texas Tech University Press for their support and advice and Robert Fink for his kind reading and generous introduction. And I especially want to thank those others who have been my mentors and friends for so many years.

Other Walt McDonald Winners

Foreword

You know the story. God has just passed judgment on the man and the woman: "Accursed be the soil because of you!" "For dust you are / and to dust you shall return." Then God casts them out of the garden of Eden. What you might not recall is that in verse twenty, chapter three of the book of *Genesis,* the man (Adam) as his last act before God posts "the great winged creatures and the fiery flashing sword, to guard the way to the tree of life," names "his wife 'Eve' [*hawwah* in Hebrew] because she was the mother of all those who live." The root of *hawwah* is *hayah* ("to live"); so Adam, having lost access to the tree of life, took Eve.

Janice Whittington's book of poetry *Into A Thousand Mouths* is the account of Eve after the fall, after she follows her husband out of the garden and into a life of tilling the soil for a yield, more often than not, of "brambles and this-tles" and, in addition for Eve, suffering "intense pain in childbearing." It is the account of one woman, of all women—

> . . . that female secret of wombs,
> the ache that folds into the chest
> and stays, a wound
> nursed into a jewel.
> ("Daughters")

The book's title is taken from the last line of the poem "Connections" and appropriately alludes to the book's pre-dominate thematic motif: women as *nurturers*. The persona of "Connections" is a new mother, three days post partum. Because her "breasts swell into fists / that open, spilling / handfuls of milk," she is taking what she hopes will be a soothing hot shower. Her breasts continue to lactate, milk sliding down her belly and legs:

Underneath my feet, eddies
swirl near the drain,
letting down
into a thousand mouths.

Not only does this Eve feed *her* baby, she sees hungry
mouths everywhere, even in the holes of the shower drain.

The connections between women and a needy world
seem to be infinite, as the five sections of the book suggest,
orchestrating and developing the connections of women to
their fathers, their mothers, their grandparents and great
grandparents, to their heritage of pioneer women, to their
displacement from the fecund East and their alienation in
the seemingly barren West, to their daughters, and to their
husbands. As nurturers, these women are also watchers,
sustainers—gentle, tough, sensuous, courageous. They are
hawwah—those who give life and live.

Section I develops the need of an adult daughter to
connect with and nurture her dying father. In "Does My
Father Dream of Sons?" the persona celebrates her father's
love for his two daughters, even though the persona believes
her father must have longed for a son, her father being "the
last of his line, / only son of an only son, / the father
of daughters." He does his best to teach his daughters and
granddaughters the ways of a male: how to shoot a twenty-
two, thread worms onto fish hooks, drive tractors, and saddle
horses, but their interests lie elsewhere: ballet, "the barn cat's
babies," "other fathers' boys." On her annual Christmas visit,
the persona and her sister leave their father dozing in his
chair, dreaming maybe of sons, and slip into the bedroom,
pile blankets on their sleeping daughters. There is always
someone to comfort.

When the father is diagnosed with cancer, his two
daughters drive the three hundred miles to be with him
for his surgery ("Highway 36"). After the surgery, they
join their mother around his bed ("All the Watchers Are
Women"). Listening to her father breathe, the persona

visualizes her connection to long lines of women who have watched over men:

> Dark-robed,
> ancient, they squat
> around the bed, mouthing
> wadded chants.

The persona finds comfort in these women: "their shadows / touch me / in the light" ("All the Watchers Are Women").

The image of light is also associated with the love and security the persona's father gave his daughter during "blizzard years in New England / when ice snapped power lines," and her father lit an oil lamp: "Daddy and I played gin for pennies, / laughing in a circle of light" ("When the Lights Fail"). His daughter now wishes to return the favor. On nights when her father is in pain, he begs his daughter to see the "ghosts of fighter pilots," his war buddies whose planes went down in "cold north seas" ("What Men Say to Each Other"). They have stepped into her father's room. She has heard him "call their names." She can only dream him "flying in the sun, / his laughter creating thermals / to keep him aloft" ("Fallen from the Sky"). Her father's ravings frighten her:

> He clenched his hand on my wrist,
> pointing to tarmac
> cluttered with pilots striding in black boots,
> wings gleaming on flight jackets.
> ("Daddy's Summer for Dying")

She is constant in her devotion. Even though she cannot see what her father, in his delirium, curses her for not seeing, she wakes in the night and drives the miles to be at his side, where the last Sunday, she hugs him, pulls him back to her for an instant and "then left him / staring at the sky" ("Daddy's Summer for Dying"). Pulling him back for that instant is her reward for such vigilance.

Section II expands her focus to life outside her family. The poems continue to celebrate women as nurturers in a world of tough beauty and deadly happenstances. The women in these poems are stronger than the men. "The Roots of Desert Plants" makes clear the toughness, the beauty of a woman who, five months from childbirth and having endured "too many miscarriages for anyone but her / to count," lies on "a slant board / in a desert hospital, feet up, / cervix sewn shut," waiting out "the trimester puffing by" so she can finally birth "the small weak thing / with wafers for lungs." Her husband isn't with her. He has too often witnessed "the flushing away," so he waits "in a dark room with strangers," drinking whiskey and "watching tight-jeaned girls / smile at him." He's getting drunk, "fearing the strength / in one woman."

In "Georgia's Canyon," the persona sees this same strength and beauty in the person and the art of Georgia O'Keeffe. O'Keeffe tramps her canyon, touching it as if it were a lover, as if her child: "Georgia / owned the land, talked to it like a lost child." Later, locked behind "the doors of her room," O'Keeffe gives birth through her art: brushes riding "her hands like hawks / soaring on thermals."

"The Carp Catchers" is my favorite poem in the collection. One woman, for months, has kept vigil over her premature baby struggling in the intensive-care unit's "clear-box" isolette. On this day, she watches from a hospital window as a woman, bowl-bearing, and with the assistance of a man, is saving carp from a drying-up playa lake. Like the mother, the woman saving carp is waging war "against gills struggling with air." We can't be sure if either of the women is winning, but we know each is fighting to sustain life.

In the third section, we are given an historical perspective on women as pioneers who left their homes in the east (specifically New England and East Texas) to follow their husbands and fathers west. Displaced from their homes, which were never far from bodies of water, these daughters and wives found themselves in Texas where "they felt the air scorch / in the sling of dust," and the rivers were "red, the land so flat / they hammered stakes on plains / to mark it theirs" ("A Wife's Place"). What they knew was the need to feed their families. They knew they must take their place: "women digging dry land, / planting."

Married to a farmer, a pioneer woman "walked behind him as he plowed, / dropping seeds in his wake" ("Land-locked"). She missed the sea. "She caught crawdads in mud banks / on strings baited with bacon." She boiled them, "adding salt, tasting shrimp / in their tough meat." This displaced New Englander "could smell storms boiling / and stowed her children in the root cellar." They rode out the storm, the mother comforting and sustaining: "Below, she hummed sailing songs, / rocking her babies to sleep."

Maybe these women never forgot the sea. A question asked in "Woman of the Sea" is whether a woman's "dream of oceans" didn't cause her to begin "wearing her hair loose," "inviting men full of salt / to sail through dangers to her arms." Maybe one day she grew tired of her hands bleeding "from lye scrubbed into shirts, / from breaking manure and cactus / into chunks for fire." When that day came, did she "step into waves of the prairie, / searching for shore / and singing?"

Most of these pioneer women pushed bonnets back, opened their mouths to the sky, its healing rain, and declared, "'Here, / here I can live'" ("Storms in Summer"). They were survivors, tough as mesquite trees: "Gnarled, bare, these trees / are the hands of prairie women" ("Mesquites in February"). The women "gripped leather straps / in birthing, buried their firstborn / killed by fever." Like the mesquites, these women were "unkillable / even by the hardest freeze." Some, however, were "beaten by childbirth and heat" ("Coyote Spring"). It is their cries we hear in the howls of coyotes.

"Horse Bones in Yellowhouse Canyon" offers a different type of connection between the women of the pioneer past and the present. This poem mourns the passing of "the tribe that loved horses," specifically celebrating the beauty and courage of this lost tribe killed in battle in the canyon.

The final stanza makes a connection between the horses, the tribe, and the poem's persona. The imagery of the final stanza depicting an Indian pony and an eminent battle is sensuous, even sexual, feminine—strength and beauty. When the persona uses the plural pronoun *our*, she could be referring to contemporary Texas women transformed by the magic of this sacred canyon into Indian ponies quivering for battle:

> Stepping over ribs, our feet
> turn to hooves stamping the dirt.
> Our skin twitches,
> the paint still damp on our flanks.
> We snort the air, ready for fists
> gripping the mane.

"Horse Bones in Yellowhouse Canyon" provides a transition to this section's concluding poems, which emphasize the female persona's affinity for the creatures of West Texas. The nurturer in the persona does not approve of what seems a male instinct for killing. She extends her concern to coyotes and seems to disapprove of their being killed, even to protect the men's Spanish goats ("The Shooter"), to sustain the men's "goat dreams" ("Coyote on the Fence"). The persona almost seems to summon the coyote ghosts "like angels / armed with swords" to swoop down upon the men, these shooters.

In the final two poems of the section, the cattle may represent displaced women. In "Salt Licks," the cattle seem dissatisfied, deserting shade to "trudge / to hollowed-out salt licks, / hungry for something missing." Here, the image may suggest that the women have fed and sustained and nurtured to the point where *they* need to be nurtured. If the poem "What It Takes" continues the implied comparison between the women and the cattle, then the implication for the women may be that their needs will go unsatisfied. Drought "burns through winter," and "men in dusty pickups / bump along fence lines / and blowtorch the prickly pear." "Cattle, their skin rawhide / strung on coat hangers, / trudge after the truck like a bellwether." Receiving only cactus for nourishment, the cattle gnaw the prickly pear and like the wife in "Woman of the Sea," "turn their backs to the wind," and maybe also, at least until the drought ends, to the men.

The last two sections shift the focus almost exclusively on the book's persona. Section IV reveals her specific longings and losses and her personal approach to sustaining herself and her family in this place she didn't choose but now claims. Section V celebrates the persona as Eve-the-mother: nurturer, sustainer.

The first half of the fourth section depicts what it is like for the persona living in West Texas. Especially in winter, she feels her New England connection "to men in plaid wool / who boil tree sap into syrup" ("Canada Geese in Texas"). Winter allows her to "forget the droughts of August, / West Texas sun that wilts crops / and melts the streets." Then comes March, and the Canada geese flock north, and West Texas farmers "dig thawed soil, / planting cotton and corn, / praying for rain."

In "Dust and Snow," the persona says that when

Texas dust
smells of burning
and rain is green dabs
on weather maps
somewhere else . . . ,

she is haunted by the cold of Wyoming. A friend writes her that "the first snows / have fallen there." The image is a sensual one: the snow is covering her friend's "peonies / with robes / soft as a lover's."

Why *wouldn't* Eve desire to escape from West Texas—a land of drought, tornadoes, hailstorms, and late frosts ("Storm Watch," "Hailstorm," "Late Frost"). Maybe she stays because at least on the plains of West Texas—the region where the persona of "More Than a Wedge of Sky" emphasizes "we live," the place she calls home—farmers can *see* the storm coming: "cumulus / roiling in domes, exploding / in white bursts." Here Eve and her family can search "for the dark finger in the distance / tracing its way, dipping down / and spinning." But she still misses Eden, craves her own jungle ("Rain Forests"). She believes "in rain forests / and lush undergrowth." She recalls her heritage—her "grandmother's gardens in East Texas" where rhododendrons grew "big as trees." She knows she must accept her Eden as being here, West Texas, where after six years the trumpet vine's roots have "finally snaked deep enough / to let us all believe / we can last here on the plains." Here, she declares, she will plant "jungles / on hardpan that burns our feet." She will create a new Eden.

Thinking of her grandmother's flower gardens draws the persona back to her East Texas bloodlines, those of her grandmother and especially her mother ("Bloodlines," "The Music of Bones," "Expensive Harvest," "Talking To Mother," "Truths About The Dead"). Hers is a heritage of stories—litanies woven together, "each voice a thread singing" ("Talking To Mother"), a paradoxical heritage of feeding and dissolution ("Bloodlines," "The Music of Bones," "Expensive Harvest," "Truths About the Dead"). She has settled into West Texas, having learned to trust the mesquites, the scissortails as the true harbingers of spring. She knows to look for signs, how long to "keep flowers / buried in rough bark" ("Late Frost") to protect them from a late, killing frost; how to nurture her garden, her husband, and her daughters.

It is fitting that the final section should begin with a love poem for the persona's husband: "His breathing / smothers the creaks I fear, / soothing my night" ("Sleeping Alone"). The wife touches the ladder of her husband's spine, checking for the rise and fall of breathing, in the same way as she would get up to check on her children when they were newborns. She sustains her family, and they sustain her: "his breath, like theirs, / folding around me / like wings."

In "Connections," the new mother is experiencing some post partum depression, but even as she struggles with the physical and psychological discomfort, she perceives her body as a source of nourishment and herself as a protector and sustainer of her child, "fragile as . . . webs pulsed across a fontanel."

"Daughters" and "For the Brave Everywhere" conclude the book by celebrating connections, the struggles of mother and daughter, "the indelible print / left beside the heart" ("Daughters"). The result is an "ache that folds into the chest / and stays," but it is a good ache, "a wound / nursed into a jewel" ("Daughters"), with emphasis on the metaphorical verb *nursed*.

The final poem, "For the Brave Everywhere," is spoken by Eve-the-life-giver after her "daughters have turned women" and sped off to the city, leaving the bare plains behind. Their mother is still here, now at peace with herself and her surroundings. She drives differently now, "slowing down on highways," watching out for the earth's creatures: "tarantulas / lured by some music / that called them to dare the span of asphalt," "frogs the rain / pulls from the earth /. . . until the pavement hops." She is watching out for life, even celebrating the courage, the daring of frogs flinging "their lives into the rain" and crossing "four lanes toward a playa lake, / ignoring wheels that could crush, / daring the pavement to burn."

This concluding image is not, obviously, just about frogs. As the poem's title states, this poem is for the brave everywhere. The lines echo the final image of "Rain Forests," where the persona and her husband have learned "to walk / barefoot on hot concrete, planting our jungles / on hardpan that burns our feet." Eve has planted her jungle west, not east of Eden, and like the trumpet vine that "shares orange buds" ("Rain Forests") and the desert plants that put down roots ("The Roots of Desert Plants"), her jungle just might flourish.

Robert Fink
Abilene, Texas, 1998

xv

Contents

IV

V

For John and Emily and Rachel

I

"He will forgive you
if the line you found was a good line.

It does not have to be worth the dying."

Milller Williams, "Let Me Tell You"

Does My Father Dream of Sons?

He taught us
to shoot a twenty-two,
to thread worms
onto fishhooks. He,
the last of his line,
only son of an only son,
the father of daughters.

We played paper dolls,
dressed his hunting dog
in pink bonnets.
We gave up horses
for ballet, gave up ballet
for boys—other fathers' boys—
then wore his old Air Force
shirts to sock hops.

At night did he dream of sons?
Strapping redheads
who corralled cattle
and mended barbed wire fences?
Six-footers who slid into cockpits
and jetted the skies, their vapor
slicing the blue?

He has granddaughters
who fish and climb trees.
He teaches them
to drive the tractor

and saddle horses,
but they wander off
to peek through cracks
at the barn cat's babies.

Our Christmas visit
iced us in, the sleet
spattering for hours. He paced,
watched television football.
The girls stirred fudge,
licking warm chocolate
from spoons.
The ice storm glazed wires
and tree limbs until they snapped.
By a dim camp lantern, he dozed
in his chair. Leaving him to his dreams,
my sister and I piled blankets
on our sleeping daughters.

Highway 36

Three hundred miles away
they wait for morning surgery
and for us to arrive.
The X rays were grim, the spot
large and dark. Mother paces.

Daddy sits on white sheets,
elbows on knees. Every few minutes
he checks his watch. Breaking all rules,
he smokes, his cigarette tip
a bright, red beacon.

In the dim green reflection
of dash light, my sister and I
are silent, listen to the radio
as miles of East Texas
roll beneath our tires.

Trees lining the road
catch our headlights and mold
a constant tunnel.
My sister drives. In a blink,
a single possum

scuttles to the center stripe,
his eyes pinpoints of light.
She brakes, swerves,
almost puts us in a ditch.
Trembling, our breathing quick,

we laugh and finally talk.
Back on the highway, we watch the road
and plan how often we will come.
The radio fades from one small town station
to another.

As the stars rotate in the night sky,
I memorize how the moon looks
as it slips down
behind the tunnel
of dark trees.

When the Lights Fail

Storms glazed Daddy's last Christmas,
ice slipping over us like a shroud.
He picked at the hair on his head
and worried the shunt near his collarbone,
his hands bruised from IVs. The next day
the girls and I drove home,
sliding for hours over interstate bridges.

This Christmas, ice wrapped holly bushes
in shawls, broke limbs off the elm out back.
House finches scratched the frost
for birdseed spilled before storms.
Huddled geese stretched necks to the wind
and watched for dogs.
Cold kept us in, working jigsaw puzzles,
finding dropped pieces on the floor
as shadows closed into evening.

Smothered in ice, transformers
exploded the night for an instant.
In the dark rooms,
we felt for familiar chairs,
the desk newly arranged in the study.
We fumbled in drawers for candles,

votives for guest bathrooms,
and Christmas decorations,
the scents of vanilla and cinnamon blending.

By candlelight we found an oil lamp
from blizzard years in New England,
when ice snapped power lines
and Daddy and I played gin for pennies,
laughing in a circle of light.

All the Watchers Are Women

At dusk I am curled in a red
Naugahyde chair,
listening to my father breathe.
I see crones.
Dark-robed,
ancient, they squat
around the bed, mouthing
wadded chants,
their lips wet, the words sputtering
down their chins
like bubbles
from wall oxygen.

They circle the bed.
Hags who have watched
before, they click
and rattle leather tongues;
their shadows
touch me
in the light.

What Men Say to Each Other

On nights when pain
strafed his head, and his only peace
a hypodermic of morphine,
ghosts of fighter pilots
strode into my father's room.
I heard him call their names,
reaching for pale hands,
for planes downed in cold north seas,
the fleece inside flight jackets
heavy with water,
words turning to gurgles
of drowning men.

Posing by airplanes sporting painted dames,
those young men grin from snapshots—
smooth-faced men with slim waists,
who wooed girls
hurried by wars
into chapels and beds,
left them to live with in-laws
and bear children in strange towns,
waiting for small folded letters
read by censors.

The young pilots of his dreams
stepped from dark lines of V-mail
and joked with him, their laughter
sweeping my father.
He begged me to see them,
these men younger than I
who flew and fell,
leaving him only their names
signed on a dollar bill

my mother found later,
tucked deep into my father's wallet,
names she barely remembered,
written in faded ink.

Fallen from the Sky

In that year doctors gave my father
as if it were a gift,
I wanted him to be
a red-tailed hawk
spinning on thermals,
stretching for another swoop

before darkness,
or that young pilot in khaki
who grinned from an old photo,
told of soaring into clouds
as flak outside the canopy
burst into bloom.

I dreamed him flying in the sun,
his laughter creating thermals
to keep him aloft,
but he sat in his old chair
with shoulders hunched
like folded wings.

His battle stories changed
as blisters filled his mouth.
I listened to him count pills,
check sputum, time
each bowel movement,
his hair thin as down,
the smell of medicine
rising from his skin
like spoiling fruit.

Daddy's Summer for Dying

I drove flat miles on Fridays,
spelling mother at the hospital.
On Four West, the dying floor,
medication sent him on night sorties.
I curled in the chair,
afraid of his ravings.

He clenched his hand on my wrist,
pointing to tarmac
cluttered with pilots striding in black boots,
wings gleaming on flight jackets.
With frothed lips, he cursed me
for not seeing ghosts.

I watched him,
fearing the visions
he shared with me, dreams
that caught him in their wings
and swept him far behind enemy lines.
Each morning, the trip back
took longer. He never remembered,
or didn't claim he did, his eyes clear
with daylight and pain.

Each weekend he left me behind,
flying higher, reaching his hands
to wave at comrades,
cursing me, his eyes furious

at my blindness.
Each breakfast, he paused
over his tray of toast or eggs,
not knowing
what to do first.

Weeks came like waves of airplanes
sweeping over me. Engines
shuddered into my sleep, and I woke
and drove the miles,
lost in some world
that curled me into corners
where my father's face grew old at dawn
but turned at nightfall
to a twenty-year-old, grinning and wild.
The last Sunday, I hugged him,
pulled him back to me for an instant,
then left him
staring at the sky.

II

"When my griefs sing to me
from the bright throats of thrushes
I sing back."

Linda Pastan, "Old Woman"

Risking the Fall

Last month, Henry leaned down for leverage
from a cherry picker bucket,
struggling with rope anchored
to a mulberry stump.
In a crash of rotten roots,
the tension snapped Henry
like a cannonball
grazing elm trees
seeing the nests of jays,
haphazard feathers and wings,
and in his ears,
the final scream of wind.

I remember Henry last summer
in the crowd at the county fair.
His small son danced
foot to foot, licking pink
sugar from fingers,
eyeing the spinning lights
and pulling on his daddy's hand.

Sweeping his son onto his shoulders,
Henry galloped away to the Tilt-A-Whirl,
and he was twelve again,
one of my sixth graders at Joyland,
ready for squeals of terror
on the roller coaster, the whip of wind
in their faces on the Bullet
when they soared,
stomachs lifting
as they plunged to the ground,
knowing at the last minute
they would be saved.

The Roots of Desert Plants

Five months from childbirth,
too many miscarriages for anyone but her
to count, a friend lay on a slant board
in a desert hospital, feet up,
cervix sewn shut,
doctors relaxing her womb
with an alcohol drip.

Nurses checked the tilt,
held mirrors as she combed
brown hair washed with corn meal
to soak up sweat and oil.
She counted hours through a haze
of mirrors and magazines
heavy as full wombs,
the trimester puffing by,
emptying finally the small weak thing
with wafers for lungs.

Too often watching the flushing away,
her husband wasn't there. Somewhere
in a dark room with strangers,
he drank whiskey,
watching tight-jeaned girls
smile at him, their eyes blurred from beer.
He hunched over the bar, getting drunk,
fearing the strength
in one woman.

Lightning

Struck by lightning years ago, Uncle Carl
doesn't feel cold anymore.
In shirt-sleeves and overalls,
he shovels snow in zero weather.

When fire streaked from the sky
and flung him to the dirt,
sparks etched his nerves,
cutting an escape. Like garden trowels,
his fingers dug into earth,
heat bursting his gloves.
He lay in the turnrow,
raindrops steaming his eyes.

He lives far off on mountains now,
tasting the cold. Wandering through birches
he burrows his hands in snow banks,
squeezing the snow
as if it were cotton.

Her hair pulled
into a knot at the base of her neck,
she took with her a piece of cedar
she'd peeled bare,
feeling the burls, the moist wood
skinned and new in her hand.
On her feet she wore those black shoes
she always wore to class
or dinner.

She tramped the canyon on burro trails,
her feet gripping steep grades, her walking pole
braced against a slide into reds hills
spotted with cedars, the white rocks
jutting like teeth from skulls.
Squatting near the ground,
she memorized cholla and spikes of buffalo grass,
felt the breeze stir the mesquites
and swept her eyes
to storms closing on the horizon
like fingers.

Sunset crept over the canyon
and took her by surprise,
the winds on the caprock
staining the sky red with dust. Georgia
owned the land, talked to it like a lost child
during vigils on the rim, and later,
when she locked the doors of her room,
brushes rode her hands like hawks
soaring on thermals.

The Carp Catchers

Through glass
that separates her from the park,
she watches rain flood the playa lake,
spawning puddles from the spillover.
Then the drying days,
when Texas sun
sucks moisture from skies
and pulls the lake back to its banks, leaving
patches of water stranded.

She stares through the window
that has caught her breath in moist circles
like fingerprints all these months. Her womb
emptied early, spilling water
and a frail coil of muscle
who struggles in a clear box.
Hourly, through portholes,
she strokes his chapped skin
as his chest shudders, sucking in and out
to the hard thump of machines.
Ten minutes of mothering,
the throb from breasts
almost dry.

She returns to the window,
sees a couple slosh to a puddle.
The woman, bowl-bearing,
steps into the marsh, stoops, then
hands the bowl to the man,
who hurries to the lake edge

and pours. The ritual repeats,
and a bright flash of orange spills out.
They are saving carp.

For a moment, she becomes the woman
cornering the slab of orange in the murk
as the fish plows mud and grass, searching
for a lost channel back, and she wages war
against gills struggling with air,
sun-crisped scales that pale and curl,
lidless eyes staring at a sky
blue as water.

Blinking, she turns from the window
toward the room with Plexiglas tanks,
and pure oxygen caught in bottles.

What Percent Water

She saw the old man's face
that first day at the tanks,
and now takes him with her
wherever she goes, like some
lost father, grandfather, uncle,
carrying him home
in the scent of her lab coat.

In her dreams the man is twenty-three,
before old age and living took his kidneys,
his bloodstream darkened with poison
no one could stop. He whispers of days
as a shrimper, hauling nets by hand,
in winter walking Galveston beaches,
the waves thudding through his veins.

Each day she works inside him, draping his body
with quiet sheets. She has touched his brain,
tracing neurons of his memories,
has reached into his chest
and held his heart. He has sired
no children but these medical students.

Today, she guides the blade,
severing torso from pelvis, then
cuts half again, each leg a new section
until he is in threes.
Baptized by bone dust,

she tastes salt in the mist,
hears the surf
singing from a shell.

III

"—and I've relearned

how paradise becomes, each year,

both something gained and something given up."

Andrew Hudgins, "Against Gardens"

A Wife's Place

When blizzards snapped apple trees,
heaved rock walls into rubble, driving wolves
into his barns, my father's grandfather
huddled by the hearth,
tracing chapped fingers over maps,
speaking trails to his wife.

With first thaw, before crocus
could urge him back,
he turned away from sunrise.
Beside him sat his wife, back straight as poplar,
her fingers bare roots pulled from earth,
her eyes snatching bits of elm and cherry,
quince limbs beginning
the flush into buds.

Leaving behind wild blueberries,
the tangle of bittersweet,
they joined other wagons
like blooms on early forsythia, the branches
curving, strung across the land.

Together they felt the air scorch
in the sling of dust. They found rivers
in Texas red, the land so flat
they hammered stakes on plains
to mark it theirs. Miles of horizon
blazed down on soddies

roofed by wagon canvas
and women digging dry land,
planting.

A child of eight,
her father brought her west
where water was red
and sand stung her cheeks like salt,
but tides surged in her pulse
as she watched the skies for squalls.

At sixteen she married a farmer
and walked behind him as he plowed,
dropping seeds in his wake.
She caught crawdads in mud banks
on strings baited with bacon, waiting for a tug,
then snapping off heads with her thumb,

boiling, adding salt, tasting shrimp
in their tough meat.
She grew loofahs on the fence,
harvesting their peeled webs for sponges
and with the mesh, scrubbed the rough off
skillets and elbows.

She could smell storms boiling
and stowed her children in the root cellar,
hearing hurricanes in tornadoes.
Outside, fences and trees washed away,
chickens like tiny ships
snagged in the trees.
Below, she hummed sailing songs,
rocking her babies to sleep.

Woman of the Sea

Did she caulk the cabin cracks
with bread dough, the dirt too hard to chip
into mud? Did wedding quilts
drag the floor, capes for one
who had packed away her veils?
Did her hands bleed
from lye scrubbed into shirts,
from breaking manure and cactus
into chunks for fire?

Did she turn her back to the wind
or lift her chin and dream of oceans,
wearing her hair loose,
bits of coral catching wisps in a red comb,
inviting men full of salt
to sail through dangers to her arms?

Did she one day
slip pins from her hair
and step into waves of the prairie,
searching for shore
and singing?

Distant thunder lumbers,
echoes of lost oxen and horses
stumbling over the plains.
Wagons sprawl like bones
in arroyos, each cutbank
a grin of madness. Clouds
vanish as they drift
like wedding veils laced with promises.

The smell of moisture
yanks horses nose up, and women
stop in the dust behind Conestogas.
Pushing bonnets back, they open mouths to the sky,
reach to the rain. "Here,
here I can live."

Arroyos roil with dark water,
quick floods
of deserts. Like mesquites,
gnarled women send taproots
deep into the Ogallala Aquifer
and wear their blossoms on bark
covered with thorns.

Mesquites in February

Thorny, deciduous mesquites
overrun West Texas. Along Highway 84
they fringe the arroyos and gullies,
clutter the distant mesas.
Gnarled, bare, these trees

are the hands of prairie women
buried by fierce winds. The twigs
are raw and rough knuckled
from scrubbing muslin shirts
and tin plates, hands callused
from plowing caliche and clay,
cactus and rocks. These hands
gripped leather straps
in birthing, buried their firstborn
killed by fever. Fingers twisted hair
into tight buns that grayed early.
Thorns planted crocus in the sand,
tatted lace for daughters' dresses,
the bone shuttles
slipping back and forth
in the firelight. These women
stretch from canyon graves
and turn to mesquites—unkillable
even by the hardest freeze.

Coyote Spring

In winds whirling up
from canyon floors,
howls ricochet off rocks,
echo the sighs of women
beaten by childbirth and heat.
Voices soak into arroyos,
stirring wildflowers in a burst of blossom
after rain, and seeds scatter
over graves of those broken
by the memory of laughter,
women who lay down
and wept their songs into sand.

Green mesas ring
with music of plains women,
beguiling coyotes
who poise
silhouetted and calling.

Horse Bones in Yellowhouse Canyon

Their thunder silent in sedge and cactus,
skulls gnawed clean, jaws
dragged off by coyotes,
the horses wait. Bottle flies and buzzards
left when the smell died.

The canyon soaked up blood of men, women,
children who galloped with sticks.
Winds whirled around burial grounds
erasing the tribe that loved horses.

Stepping over ribs, our feet
turn to hooves stamping the dirt.
Our skin twitches,
the paint still damp on our flanks.
We snort the air, ready for fists
gripping the mane.

Seeing the coyote slung on the fence,
I wonder if one evening the rancher
pulled red shells from his pocket
and tapped them for luck?
Did he hide in the hay, holding his breath
as a skunk ambled by in the dark?
Was he lulled by rumblings
of Spanish goats shaking chin whiskers
and butting? Did he listen
for distant howls of coyotes

or simply wait, the barn wood
shrunk enough
to fit a barrel through?

After midnight, maybe the moon
caught the flick of tail,
the flash of teeth,
shotgun.

Bent down and staring
at moonlight on damp fur,
did he crush spent shells into dust
and shove the goats away?

Coyote on the Fence

The head hangs,
all that's left of the carcass
draped on barbed wire by farmers
wanting to frighten coyotes away
like angels of death.
The skin shrinks in the sun,
peeling from bone in a grimace
of teeth once wet with flesh
and blood of goats.

Night wind spins through hollows
of the skull, the hide curling into wings.
Howls brush across men,
skimming their goat dreams
like angels
armed with swords.

Feral

Wild hogs saunter beside Highway 62,
wander into the brush
as if we don't matter,
as if they own the Breaks,
land that earned its name,
strewn with wagons abandoned
like sloughed snake skins,
its arroyos cut for hooves
or sinuous bellies rubbing against sandstone
in hard rattles.

Dumped a generation ago
from Georgia wagons swallowed by sand,
some hogs withered,
but others ran squalling in the heat
and dug into shade.
Now wild hogs own the breaks, their hides
tough, ignoring mesquite thorns and scrub.

At night, they skulk near asphalt,
luring sharp-sighted young men
who wear tight Levis
and starched shirts, those
who strut their chests in Dodge trucks
with duals and a gun rack in the rear window,
ease through the backwoods on moonlit nights,
hands wrapped around longnecks
or thighs of blondes with big hair,
searching the breaks
for hogs.

Salt Licks

Goats crowd liquid-feed boxes,
tongues spin wheels,
lifting the juice,

but cattle shrug
under mesquite thorns
and plod to the salt licks,
yellow chunks
in pastures.

Tongues scrape the squares,
wearing down corners. They are the winds
eroding mountains to spikes of sandstone,
scooping caves from cliffs
with rough licks,
the bedrock honeycombed
with dens for rattlers.

Deserting shade, cattle trudge
to hollowed-out salt licks,
hungry for something missing.

The ground splits in August,
and pastures scorch into stubble.
Windmill blades
clatter like heartbeats,
dredging up water in spurts.

By autumn the lake shrinks,
ringed with mud drying into dust,
and thirsty cattle nose brown water.
Bass share murk with mud cats,
slide closer to the deep end near the dam,
the shallows
swallowed by Texas sun.

As drought burns through winter,
men in dusty pickups
bump along fence lines
and blowtorch the prickly pear,
the blue flames scalding away spines.
Cattle, their skin rawhide
strung on coat hangers,
trudge after the truck like a bellwether,
gnaw the cactus,
turn their backs to the wind.

IV

"Elsewhere the sky is the roof of the world;

but here the earth was the floor of the sky."

Willa Cather, *Death Comes for the Archbishop*

Winter in a West Texas Town

Two lean hounds
lope out of Johnson grass,
then pad along the pavement
toward town, heads drooped,
long strides matching.
Elms border the road's north side,
flapping snagged plastic in the wind.
Cedars and pyracantha
camouflage the peeling paint
of clapboard houses. On the lawns,
ceramic gnomes and ducks,
covered in cotton fuzz from the local co-op,
pose in a halted parade.

Parked at Odom's feed store,
one old green pickup, its antenna
a coat hanger. Two doors down,
farmers in bib overalls,
stained baseball caps and plaid coats
converge at the gas station,
check the weather
and spit.
Four blocks away
from all directions
tumbleweeds
bounce into town.

During Alberta clippers
when wind wheels winter to us,
the lakes freeze
from edge to center,
crowding Canada geese together
in a dark thatch of noise
wrinkling the water.

Lured by their clatter
breaking the dry air,
we stir from hibernation
inside insulated walls
and bundle into heavy coats
to walk the lake shore.

Geese bunch into clumps,
dipping heads into water like corks
on fishing poles. At a silent signal,
flocks scurry across the water,
whole battalions
rising on wings.
Others stroll the bank,
their black necks
stiff as walking canes,
or stoop into humps
pecking bread crumbs and corn.

They bring us out into winter,
connect us to men in plaid wool
who boil tree sap into syrup
up north where summer mountains

wear dust whiter than caliche.
We forget the droughts of August,
West Texas sun that wilts crops
and melts the streets.

In March the ice slides back
and playa lakes steam,
moisture lifting
like fog. Then the geese
flock north
where lakes hold a skim of ice,
and for months, we dig thawed soil,
planting cotton and corn,
praying for rain.

The Arrowhead

Rachel scouted the back pasture
after Papa Whit's plowing
and found an arrowhead.
Tying it in a red bandanna,
she climbed on Old Blue
bareback, urging him
into an easy lope home.

Geese settled in the lake reeds,
and she sat cross-legged
on the porch, turning the flint,
catching the low sun
on its sharp edges.

Arrowhead under her pillow,
she slept. Rattled songs of lake frogs,
low, double notes of doves
drifted through the screened windows,
and the evening sky
drummed with the echoes
of summer thunder.

Dust and Snow

Texas dust
smells of burning
and rain is green dabs
on weather maps
somewhere else. Wyoming
haunts me. I dream
of winds
that whirled ghost dances,
blizzards
sweeping the dark highway,
of mornings
burst open so blue
my eyes ached, and nights
when stars streaked into my hands,
burning with frost.

A friend writes
the first snows
have fallen there,
covering her peonies
with robes
soft as a lover's.

More Than a Wedge of Sky

I.

Sunsets start early
on the plains where we live,
dust in the sky
a prism bending the light
red. Rising heat
molds the sun
into a fluted medallion
mirroring faces
that stare at the horizon
unafraid.

II.

When we head west
to Sangre de Cristo mountains,
climbing beyond the caprock
on a road that undulates
like a sunning snake,
we stumble,
squinting in valleys
when the sun falls into pines,
spilling night around us.
We can't find east,
and storms ambush us from forests,
pounding down mountains
like surprise.

III.

At home, before radar warns us,
we see cumulus
roiling in domes, exploding
in white bursts
until the ledge cloud tops the storm.
We watch for the red wall
rumbling dirt from three counties west,
and often we look up, searching
for the dark finger in the distance
tracing its way, dipping down
and spinning.

We plant cedar windbreaks
around clapboard houses,
but nothing stops the wind
on caprock horizons
where settlers hammered
stakes into the ground as landmarks.

Russian thistles roll,
tumbling skeleton-elbows and ribs
curled inward. Stunted crabapples
shove roots through layers of stone,
thirsting for the Ogallala Aquifer.
Each season, they bloom,
branches twisting
away from the wind.

The sky fell last night.
Chunks of hard clouds
careened to earth. Cowering
under the slam of stones,
we covered our ears
as hail like arguments
crashed around us. Texas stories
of hailstones big as softballs,
a braggart's story, turned real.
Cars shuddered, bloomed in sharp flowers,
their windows burst out, the glass lying
like tears. Roofs shredded and skylights
gaped like mouths asking why.

Horses died where they stood,
their huge eyes soft with questions,
as hailstones, pale peaches, piled up
beneath stripped trees.

Drawn to sheltered windows
like mesmerized moths,
we watched the debris
of crashing glass and limbs,
prayed for those left outside
and for ourselves bearing the losses.

When the high plains bloom,
mesquite buds
clench like fists.
Freezing winds sting blossoms,
robbing the purse of fruit.

In spring, I hesitate to believe,
wear sweaters through March.
Into April my gloves lie
on the floorboard of the car,
ready for the snap

that frosts the windshield.
Apricots and pears bloom early,
throw blossoms open to April sun.
Here on the caprock, I watch the skies
for dark threads. Like the mesquites,

I keep flowers
buried in rough bark until
scissortails spin through the sky,
believing their wings.

On these high plains where
rain clouds split over the city
or hit the caprock and dissipate,
leaving us dry, I crave my own jungle.

Believing in rain forests
and lush undergrowth,
I argue with dirt and dust,
ignore zone numbers in magazines,
and each spring
scatter poppy seeds that never sprout.
I long for peonies and clematis,
the cool of deep-wood ferns
and mist rising after the sun sinks,
recall my grandmother's gardens in East Texas
where rhododendrons big as trees
formed backdrops for Easter pictures
and dogwoods held their blossoms
like teacakes stacked.

But my gardens grow gourds with white blooms
that come out at dusk
and drop off when sun strikes them.
Out back, morning glories
drape blue over a tripod of branches
tied and stuck into clay.
And after six years, the trumpet vine
shares orange buds,

the roots finally snaked deep enough
to let us all believe
we can last here on the plains
where wind whips our hair into shredded blossoms
and dust clouds roil. Here we learn to walk
barefoot on hot concrete, planting our jungles
on hardpan that burns our feet.

Fish heads on the fence
in East Texas legend
whisper *incest,*
idiots inside.

Snagged on rusted fence wire
by the upper lip,
yellowed catfish heads
yawn, mouths big enough
to swallow a thermos of whiskey in one gulp.
Smaller heads hang
with dying crusts of skin.

Flesh spilling like dough
from her sleeves, Grandma Frazier
rocks on the porch swing, stabbing her words
with a toothpick.

She tells of kin who spread west from Georgia
like kudzu, herding hogs to chase snakes,
how men with my name
squatted by ponds and dropped hooks,
then slaughtered the Hampshires.
Bacon grease fried the fish,
and chunks of fat lured
crawdads from creek banks.

A catfish caught
on a trotline of stories,
I fight deep currents of mossy lakes,

struggle against the hook
lodged in my gill.

From white-bellied uncles,
double cousins
hang gape-jawed on the fence,
and I gasp for air,
feel swamp water sliding off my skin,
the slow haul of the line.

The Music of Bones

Mother wanted the shinnery oak
trimmed by the fence line. All day
chips in my eyes,

the pockets of my blouse, chain oil
spattered my face, my arms bled
from limbs falling the wrong way.

Coyotes woke me
from darkness I know
only at the farm, the night filled with owls,

their voices dark wings against the moon.
Shadows scraped window screens, and howls
drew copper on my tongue.

Next morning we checked the boneyard,
found the coyotes had feasted
on the old cow with low potassium

who wobbled, sat down, and died.
Our truck scattered slow turkey vultures
who lumbered up

steep steps of air.
We scanned the back of the carcass

for signs, ignoring the savage
softness of eye and underbelly.

Hot and white like bones, the noon sky
uprighted the night's bowl of black,
revealed more brush to trim.

Years away, in the clutter of my desk
rest collected farm skulls—
armadillo, skunk, goat—

on city nights, bones
that tremble in my hands
the echoes
of a coyote's wail.

Expensive Harvest

Six crows raid my mother's orchard.
On ripe mornings
they stab into juicy peach and plum,
then flap away in a cackle.
Mother drapes nets over the branches,
later finds gouged peaches
and a tangled scissortail.
She coils long plastic snakes
through fruit-heavy limbs,
scaring off only rabbits
and grandchildren.

Today she stacks red shotgun shells
next to bushel baskets,
watches the crows
wheel above her trees
in raucous pirouettes.

Every time I call her,
murmurs of other women
haunt the wires,
women who sit and wait
for phone calls on Sunday afternoons
when hours unravel
and the sun loiters in the sky.
They hear me dial
and tap into the line between mother
and me. I hear them whisper

stories of grandsons
who streak to victory in track meets,
daughters who sew perfect collars,
and dead husbands who took them square dancing,
petticoats red and whirling.
Their litanies weave together,
each voice a thread singing.
Shuttles click against each other,
taking turns, catching
my phone wire in the cloth.

Through the white princess phone,
my mother speaks with their voices,
and when she hangs up,
the silence on the line
echoes like sighs.

Truths About the Dead

My grandmother's words
turned to whips, stinging us back to her.
Each time we left, she whispered in our ears,
warned us for thirty years,
she'd soon be dead,
pulling us down East Texas blacktop
to red dirt and pines. My father
came back, her son paying debts,
hands jingling change in his pockets.

I took her my child like a payment,
first of the fourth generation.
In a photo my father frowns,
and I am a young woman
holding a baby. Beside me
my grandmother's eyes
are coins of reflected light.
Mouth open, she whispers in my ear.

From here, I cannot
recall her words. Caught
in the silence of the picture,
she is a withered vine
clinging to my father and me,
not the woman who scolded us
for not living nearer,
giving us as we left
the heavy baggage
of her good-byes.

V

"To have been one

of many ribs

and to be chosen."

Linda Pastan, "Aspects of Eve"

Sleeping Alone

I leave the closet light on
when I sleep alone,
the door open a crack,
fearing not thieves
but darkness.
The night shudders with noises,
and I wake tangled
in sheets and sounds not there
when my husband
lies beside me.

His breathing
smothers the creaks I fear,
soothing my night. Awaking,
I touch the ladder of his spine,
as I did checking my children
when as newborns they slept
separate from me
in cribs too large for those
accustomed to wombs.

I feel for the rise and fall
against my hand,
his breath, like theirs,
folding around me
like wings.

Three days post partum
my breasts swell into fists
that open, spilling
handfuls of milk—
the letting down, books call it.

My chest aches, trying to synchronize
with cat-mews of a stranger.
The tangle of flesh
that tore loose
and flushed out of me
now trips wires
that trigger floods.

In the shower, hot water
soothes my breasts.
Milk slides down my belly
and legs, forming
the curve of an ear
fragile as spring narcissus,
the moon slivered into a thumbnail,
webs pulsed across a fontanel.
Underneath my feet, eddies
swirl near the drain,
letting down
into a thousand mouths.

Mothering

At four months,
the flutter of fetus,
the stirring
that changes who I am.

Later, the push,
shoulders slipping out,
the tearing away of placenta,
that garden my body created
like paradise.

With scissors snips,
the letting go begins.
A tangle of arms and legs
flushes into cries, a wet fist
clenches my finger,
first steps on a journey
of forever
tearing away.

Daughters

I look at photographs and wonder,
who is the short woman
standing there between them?
From far away their voices
laugh through wires,
and we interlace words
like fingers.

I remember origami wings
fluttering in my womb, those early
stretching kicks I put my hand to,
knowing by the toes dug under my ribs
that these were girls.
The push against my body
foretold the struggles
of mother and daughter,
the indelible print
left beside the heart,
bruised forever on the rib,
marking the place where
they, too, will feel toes of daughters
curling, that female secret of wombs,
the ache that folds into the chest
and stays, a wound
nursed into a jewel.

For the Brave Everywhere

When the girls were small,
we drove the back road
between Seymour and Archer City
one spring evening
when the road crawled with tarantulas
lured by some music
that called them to dare the span of asphalt,
ours the only car, the only wheels
to stop their trek.

Now, daughters have turned women
and speed through cutbanks
molded from concrete, living near skyscrapers
these bare plains don't grow
or oceans in the lowlands where moisture
veils loblolly pines.

And I drive differently,
slowing down on highways.
I watch for spiders
called by music I don't hear,
or frogs the rain
pulls from the earth
like rabbits from magicians' hats
until the pavement hops.
Frogs bloom with summer storms,
like cactus in the desert.
They fling their lives into the rain,

leap for air and cross four lanes toward a playa lake,
ignoring wheels that could crush,
daring the pavement to burn.

Selected by Robert Fink, *Into a Thousand Mouths* is the eighth winner of the Walt McDonald First-Book Competition in Poetry. The Competition is supported generously through donated subscriptions from *The American Scholar, The Atlantic Monthly, The Georgia Review, The Hudson Review, The Massachusetts Review, Poetry,* and *The Southern Review.*